ALL THINGS FOXES FOR KIDS

FILLED WITH PLENTY OF FACTS, PHOTOS, AND FUN TO LEARN ALL ABOUT FOXES

ANIMAL READS

WWW.ANIMALREADS.COM

THIS BOOK BELONGS TO...

_____

_____

WWW.ANIMALREADS.COM

CONTENTS

Welcome to the Cunning World of Foxes!	1
What Are Foxes?	7
Different Species of Foxes	13
History of Foxes	33
Characteristics and Appearance	37
The Life Cycle of Foxes	53
Let's Howl Through the Sounds of a Fox	59
The Importance of Foxes	63
Thank You!	69

WELCOME TO THE CUNNING WORLD OF FOXES!

Beautiful, clever, resourceful, and adaptable: these are just some of the adjectives used to describe a fox.

Foxes are incredible animals that are universally loved. Aside from being utterly adorable, foxes are known to be inquisitive, fun-loving, and playful. For these and many more reasons, they have been featured in children's books and stories for generations, from *The Fox and the Hound* and *Fox in Socks* to *The Fantastic Mr. Fox* and so many others.

Foxes are famous for being incredibly clever. Have you ever heard the expression '*sly as a fox*'?

Adults use this expression often to describe someone who is cunning and smart, *just like a fox!* Sometimes, a fox will use clever tricks to outsmart prey or predator. This is just as well, given foxes all over the world have had to adapt to a rapidly changing environment.

Once upon a time, foxes had plenty of wilderness to roam and thrive. Today, as mankind encroaches on nature to build ever-growing cities and highways, foxes have had to adapt. In the last few years, foxes have had to sneak into inhabited areas and steal food, which is how they earned their reputation for being sneaky thieves. But, in reality, this is a clever animal that has had to change over the years to keep up with the booming human population on this planet.

These small, smart, fast, and agile animals are truly impressive. **They can run as fast as 40 miles per hour, climb trees, dig underground dens, and go nuts over blueberries!**

Are you keen to dive into the fox world and learn all there is to know about this magnificent and fascinating animal?

Then join us!

Let's all enter the magical world of foxes. Let's be super-duper quiet and calm, and see, if just once, we can sneak up on one and learn all its marvelous tricks.

WHAT ARE FOXES?

Foxes are small and furry animals with pointy ears and incredibly fluffy tails. They are members of the **Canidae** or 'dog' family, which includes all domesticated dogs, plus wolves, coyotes, and jackals.

There are around 20 distinct species of fox in the world, and it is one of the most varied canine families. They range in weight between two and 24 pounds, so they are classified as small-to-medium-sized canines. Aside from humans, foxes have the widest distribution of any mammals on the planet, which means they are found on every continent except Antarctica. They typically live in holes or dens which they dug themselves or have been dug by other animals, such as badgers or ground squirrels. Living in dens means foxes can easily hide from bigger predators.

Unlike many other canine species, foxes lead a mostly solitary life. Some species live in packs, with as many as 20 members. Each one has a specific role within their family group, such as hunter, lookout, or caretaker of small pups. Solitary species, on the other hand, only come together to mate, play or share a nice grooming session.

FUN FACT: The word "fox" derives from the Old English word "foc," which means "thief." This name was given because of the fox's natural ability to snatch food from its predators

Foxes are **omnivores**, so they eat both plants and animals. They like to hunt small mammals like rodents or rabbits but can eat almost anything they find, including fish, frogs, birds, and small mammals. When food is scarce, foxes may also eat nuts, seeds, or even insects such as ants. Just like you, they also eat fruits, and one of their favorites is blueberries.

Aside from looking spectacular, a fox's bushy tail is one of its most useful traits, as it helps it keep balance when running or jumping. Their fur is usually reddish-brown or gray, but it can be black too! Both males and females have short, pointed snouts with long whiskers on each side of their faces. Whiskers help a fox detect movement nearby, even before they see anything. *Think you could ever sneak up on a fox?* **Think again!** These amazing animals will know you are there long before *you* know *they* are there.

Foxes are exceptional swimmers and can stay in water for up to half an hour! Some foxes will even catch fish by swimming into shallow water with their mouths open wide enough so that fish can't see them coming until it's too late. *How clever is that?*

The most interesting thing about foxes is that they usually roam around and hunt at night. It is because this is when they see better than during the day. That is why they are called **nocturnal animals**. They are active at night and sleep during the day!

I'LL TAIL YA WHAT...

DIFFERENT SPECIES OF FOXES

You might have heard of the red fox or fennec fox, but these are just two examples of these cute animals. Some of them live in cold climates like Europe, Asia, or Canada, while others can be found in places like Eastern Africa, Australia, and South America. You're sure to find at least one type of fox that will become your favorite!

The classification of foxes is a little bit tricky. There are 6 *genera* of fox with over 37 species, ranging from small size to slightly large size. The most common genera are the *Vulpes*, also known as *true foxes,* and *Lycalopex*, or *South American foxes*. Each type is unique, but they are all related and have similar appearances and behavior.

So, let's go on a fox safari and meet some of the cutest, most unique foxes out there!

FUN FACT: Foxes eat small amounts at each meal because they have very tiny stomachs. If they manage to catch large prey, they will bury the remains of their hoard in the forest and get back to it later on.

Vulpes' True' Foxes

Preferring to go unnoticed, true foxes are immensely cunning and beautiful creatures. Like most foxes, Vulpes stay aloof by day, but at night, they go out to look for food and dance to find a mate. They live shorter lives than most other types of canines. They are also much smaller in size.

There are 12 species of true foxes. Below are some of them:

THE RED FOX

As its name suggests, red foxes are mostly golden-red in color with black legs and white fur around their muzzle. They are considered by many to be one of North America's most enchanting wild animals, with tails that are almost two-thirds the length of their entire body.

This is the largest fox species in the world.

These outstanding animals are so gifted that animal experts think of them as the ultimate triathletes: they can jump a 6-foot fence, run over 30 miles an hour, and swim superbly. What's more, they have superhuman hearing. A red fox can hear the faintest mouse squeak from as far away as 110 yards.

This is one of the solitary species of fox, who choose just one mate for life (*they are* **monogamous**) and live in pairs or tiny family groups. When they head out to hunt, however, they always hunt alone.

Red foxes average about 10 pounds in weight and about 40 inches in length. They eat small animals like mice, but they will also eat fruit if they find some on the ground. They live in forests or wooded areas where there's plenty of food available for them to eat, like berries from trees.

Female red foxes usually give birth to 2-4 **kits** (*baby foxes*) each summer and have been known to only live for 3-4 years in the wild.

BENGAL OR INDIAN FOX

The Bengal fox has a short grayish coat and much shorter and smaller legs than the red fox, although its tail is just as fluffy.

This stunning fox species is found only in the Indian subcontinent and is a medium-sized species that also lives as a bonded pair. Bengals prefer to live in areas with short grass, so they favor mountainous foothills and semi-dry deserts. When pups come along (*usually 3-6 kits*), both mom and dad will care for them.

Bengal foxes are pretty widespread in the Indian subcontinent, and although their exact numbers are unknown, experts are not too worried about their safety. Nevertheless, Bengal foxes are threatened by hunting and habitat loss.

CAPE FOX

Also known as a silver-backed jackal, the Cape fox is native to the southern regions of Africa, right around the southern cape of the continent.

This is a small fox species, usually only 34 inches in length and weighing around 10 pounds. When newborn, a Cape fox kit will weigh about 3 ounces! They have large pointy ears that look totally oversized for their tiny frame.

The Cape's fur tends to be grey around the top of the body, with slight yellowing on the sides. They have very slender legs and an adorable black tip on their very bushy tail.

Sadly, this animal is hunted for its fur, which is still used to make fox fur capes. It also falls prey to automobile accidents and canine diseases like rabies and distemper. Unfortunately, the Cape fox is often mistaken for jackals, and farmers consider them a threat to livestock. Despite these threats, animal conservationists don't consider this species to be under threat. Currently, an estimated 31,000 Cape foxes are living in the wild.

TIBETAN SAND FOX

The Tibetan sand fox is widely considered to be one of the world's rarest animals. Calm and gentle, this fox species prefers to be left alone and is described as being very shy and cute.

As their name suggests, Tibetan sand foxes inhabit the high grasslands of the Tibetan Plateau of China, Nepal, and Bhutan. Here, they hunt herds of marmots, pikas, and hares. They can also scavenge musk deer, Tibetan antelopes, and blue sheep carcasses.

The Tibetan sand fox is a fierce-looking animal with an intense stare, large build, and stunning red and gray fur. Since they live in the windswept Tibetan tundra, they have evolved to have stocky, furry bodies with particularly short legs. Being lower to the ground means this fox can better handle high winds. Its fluffy coat helps it cope with very low winter temperatures.

KIT FOX

The smallest canine species in North America, the Kit for is insanely cute and boasts a small body, large ears, and an endearing muzzle. A dog-like fox that loves to hunt alone at night in the shrublands of the southwestern United States and northern Mexico. A voracious and opportunistic hunter, this fox species hunts Merriam's kangaroo rats, prairie dogs, black-tailed jackrabbits, and plants.

Only a foot-and-a-half long, the Kit fox is a sociable animal that prefers to live in groups and is believed to live up to 12 years in the wild. This fox prefers to live in desert areas and has therefore evolved to have very large ears, which helps the animal literally let off steam. Amazingly, they also have the ability to go without fresh water to drink – all the hydration this animal needs, it gets from its food.

ARCTIC FOX

Sleek, agile, tough, and breathtaking, the Arctic fox is undoubtedly one of the most beautiful creatures on earth. Their fluffy blinding-white fur helps the animal camouflage in the icy terrain it calls home: the Arctic is the northernmost region of our planet and one of the least hospitable places for any animal to live. The fur's color changes throughout the year – from white to grey – so the fox can always blend into its surroundings.

With a small and compact body that retains heat, the Arctic fox can live in temperatures of -58

Fahrenheit. This fascinating animal has survived, against all odds, for eons. In Iceland, it is the only native wild animal, dealing with harsh natural conditions that have made it perhaps the hardiest creature on earth.

FENNEC FOX

Yes, we know, all foxes are simply adorable. *But have you laid eyes on a Fennec yet?!*

With ears that make up almost half its body length, the Fennec is one of the most unique fox species around. The smallest of all the fox species, the Fennec is native to northern Africa and is loved primarily for its humongous ears. Those oversized ears serve two useful purposes: to detect the movement of animals living underground (*food time!*) and, as will all desert-dwelling foxes, to release excess heat from their bodies.

Apparently, if you live in hot climates, you will need very big ears to keep cool!

Unsurprisingly, the Fennec has the largest ear-to-body-size ratio of any canine in the world.

Lycalopex or South American 'False' Foxes

The South American continent is home to several species of fox.

Here are the most common ones:

HOARY FOX

Found in Brazil, the Hoary fox is an agile hunter that sports a gray coat with a yellowish-white belly. They're known for their friendly nature and distinctive orange eyes. When the sun goes down, this unique fox species springs into action, ready to scavenge for food and hunt for any small rodents, dung beetles, or termites that cross their path.

Unlike most other fox species, the Hoary feeds mainly on insects – that's probably because this is known as a *'false fox*,' or a canine that is most closely related to jackals. With a height of 25 inches and weighing only around 8 pounds, the Hoary is a small canine that is under threat. Currently, only around 18,000 are found in the wild.

PAMPAS OR AZARA'S FOX

Named after the Pampas regions, this fox species thrives throughout parts of Argentina, Brazil, and Peru. They are known as large-eared dogs and are found in grasslands, where they patiently stalk their prey. They are very social and active both during the day and night and, unlike most true foxes, prefer to hunt in packs!

GENUS UROCYON

There are two species in the genus Urocyon: The gray fox and the island fox. What's interesting is that researchers have identified them as the ancestors of the entire canine family. This means that all living canines may have evolved from these fox species!

THE GRAY FOX

The gray fox is one of the most common types of foxes in North America. They can be found in forested areas and grasslands, where they survive on small animals like birds and rodents. They are also known as the American Red Fox or the Swamp Fox because they live near water sources such as swamps and rivers. The gray fox has a distinctive white tip at the end of its tail; this feature helps it hide from predators while hunting prey at night when it's dark outside!

ISLAND FOX

This adorable fox is an endearing species that inhabits the Californian Channel Islands. It is one of the smallest canine species in North America. Despite its size, it's still unmistakable with its short legs, small ears, and speckled color scheme. Unfortunately, the species is listed as endangered.

WHAT DO YOU CALL A FOX WITH NO LEGS?

A <u>FUR</u>ball!

HISTORY OF FOXES

The history of foxes is long and complicated, and it's hard to pinpoint exactly when they first appeared on Earth. But we do know they were around at least 30 million years ago! They have been part of human culture for thousands of years, dating back to ancient Egypt and Greece. They have also been tamed and kept as pets since ancient times.

According to stories, foxes first appeared in Europe about 10 million years ago and became widespread across other continents like Asia. They were among the first animals to be domesticated by humans, who began keeping them as pets around 10,000 years ago. It's not clear exactly how foxes became popular pets in Europe. Some historians believe that the rise in popularity may be linked to Queen Victoria's love of them! The animals were often kept as pets by wealthy families who could afford them; some even had their own servants dedicated exclusively to looking after their foxes and making sure that they were well cared for.

Foxes have been found in a fossilized form on every continent except Antarctica, though their populations have dwindled over time because of habitat loss and hunting. Today, most species live in forests or grasslands, but some live in deserts or mountains.

Did you know that foxes love to play as you do? In fact, they are very playful and highly social animals. They love to chase each other around, wrestle with each other, and even play in the water.

Playing is a great way for them to develop coordination and learn how to live in their environment, so they need to do it regularly. Foxes will often roll around in leaves or grass before eating it. This helps them clean their fur and get rid of any bugs that may be on their body.

WHAT'S A FOX'S FAVORITE BEVERAGE?

A <u>FUR</u>-appuccino!

CHARACTERISTICS AND APPEARANCE

Foxes are amazing animals. They're a little bit like dogs, but they have their own distinct personalities and characteristics. They're so much more than just the furry little critters popping up in children's stories.

Let's learn what makes foxes special with their characteristics and features below.

FOXES HAVE BIG EARS

First off, foxes have big ears. These big ears help them hear sounds over long distances — and since they're nocturnal, they rely on hearing more than sight to find food during the night.

Their ears are also pointed forward, which helps them hear prey while they're running at full speed through the woods.

FOXES HAVE SMALL POINTY FACES

Because they have pointed faces with a long, narrow snouts, foxes can gain entry into small burrows and holes and can easily dig out yummy critters to eat.

FOXES HAVE BUSHY AND LONG TAILS

When most people think of a fox, they imagine a cute little animal running around with that magnificent bushy tail sticking up in the air. Their tails are very bushy and full of fur — the more hair there is on their tail, the better it will work as an airfoil when they run.

Airfoils help keep things moving forward. They use their long tails to keep their balance when they run. Without their long, bushy tails, they will trip over if they try to run too fast!

FOXES HAVE SHARP TEETH AND CLAWS

Sharp teeth and claws are useful for foxes to catch their prey. If you've ever seen a fox chase down a rabbit, you might have wondered how it does it: after all, **rabbits are much faster than foxes!** But the trick is in the paws! When a fox chases down a rabbit, it uses its strong front paws to grab and hold onto the rabbit while its hind legs kick out and catch up with the front ones. This allows the fox to catch up with its prey quickly and easily!

FOXES HAVE A BEAUTIFUL, THICK COAT

From reddish-brown to gray and white, foxes have unique, warm, and fuzzy coats. *You know how the cold just seems to get into your bones and make you shiver?* Well, foxes don't have that problem. They have fluffy fur coats, which help them to stay warm in even the most frigid of temperatures. This is one of the reasons they can be active during the winter months — they don't need to hibernate! Their fur also insulates them from heat loss when running at high speeds.

As you have learned by now, the fluffiest foxes live in the coldest climates, and species that live in hot areas tend to have much shorter fur.

FOXES HAVE WHISKERS

Have you ever noticed that foxes have whiskers? Like cats, foxes have whiskers too. Their whiskers help foxes detect changes in their environment by feeling vibrations in the air around them. This allows them to hunt for food more effectively! They also use their whiskers to communicate with each other. For example, a fox will wiggle its whiskers when it wants another fox to come closer.

More Fascinating Fox Characteristics!

MOST FOXES ARE NOCTURNAL

Most types of foxes are nocturnal. It means they sleep during the day and come out at night when it's dark. They also have an acute sense of sight, which is why you're not likely to see one by day. Their eyesight is best at night. They will come out at night and search for food because they know their prey is out, so their chance of catching a yummy meal is higher. Plus, they want to roam when it is dark to avoid their predators. However, some species also often hunt at dawn or dusk (*diurnal*) or some in the day, like the Tibetan foxes.

FOXES ARE MAMMALS

A fox is a mammal, which means they feed their babies with milk from their mother. They are vertebrates that are distinguished by their fur and ability to produce live young.

FOXES ARE TERRITORIAL ANIMALS

Foxes have specific territories where they live and roam. They mark their territory by urinating and defecating on objects to leave their scent. In fact, they're so territorial that they can even fight off larger animals like dogs and coyotes when they feel threatened. They will chase other foxes out of their territory if they come across them while they are looking for food or shelter.

Unique Features and Characteristics

FOXES HAVE EXTREMELY LIGHTWEIGHT BODIES

Have you ever been weighed on a scale? How heavy are you? Being heavy is not a thing for foxes! They need to have extremely lightweight bodies to move quickly, jump, and run fast to catch their prey. Their bones are very thin, which makes them flexible and strong.

So, the next time you see a fox hopping around, be sure to praise them for being such an incredible athlete!

FOXES HAVE EXCELLENT SENSES OF SMELL AND HEARING

Foxes have excellent senses of smell and hearing — and even eyesight. They use their eyesight to find food and detect danger, but it's their sense of smell that makes them such efficient hunters.

A fox's powerful nose can smell something up to a mile away and can hear sounds from a distance up to 5 miles away! If a fox smells a rabbit or other small animal hiding in the grass, it will dig up the ground with its paws until it finds its prey. They make sure they don't miss any delicious morsels!

SOME FOXES CAN JUMP HIGH

According to studies, some species (*like the red fox*) can jump over very high obstacles. Their jumping ability also helps them use obstacles to escape when they are being chased. Their tails are long and muscular, which allows them to propel themselves into the air. They also have strong legs and back muscles, which help them leap with ease.

How about you, how high can you jump?

FOXES ARE VERY GOOD AT CLIMBING TREES

Their paws have large pads with soft fur between them, which helps them grip branches better than other animals of similar size. They can climb trees so quickly that it's hard to keep track of exactly where they are going!

FOX HABITAT

Foxes live in dens called earths or burrows that they dig with their sharp claws. They also use grasses and leaves to cover their den, so they can remain hidden from predators during the day. They may also dig dens under tree stumps or logs where they can rest safely at night.

WHERE DID THE FOX GO TO BUY A NEW TAIL?

To the re-<u>TAIL</u> store!

THE LIFE CYCLE OF FOXES

The life cycle of a fox is a fascinating journey from birth to adulthood. Their lifespan is not long, but it's packed with action!

A female fox is what you call a **vixen**. Interestingly, a male fox is also called a **dog** (sometimes, tod or reynard). Foxes mate for life and will raise their young together as a family unit. The litter usually consists of two or three **kits** that stay with their parents until they are old enough to leave home (usually by around *six months*).

Foxes are known for their unique calls, which can sound like rusty hinges on an old barn door.

On a cold winter night, you can listen for foxes from miles away as they release their mating calls into the night.

You can probably think of many species of foxes, but did you know that they don't all breed at the same time? Most species breed during the winter and have their litters in spring. After the vixen gives birth, the male fox remains with them for about 40 days to help raise their babies until they are weaned.

The fox goes through several phases, starting from **infancy** to **adolescence** and **adulthood**.

INFANCY

When a vixen and a male fox mate, they produce cute little foxes called *litters* or *kits*. At birth, the kits will still have their eyes closed. They will be unable to walk on their own and rely on their mother for food and protection from predators. The mother fox will also teach her kits basic skills like how to hunt for food or how to navigate their habitat safely. Once she feels like her pups are ready, she will leave them behind so they can go out into the world alone and learn to be independent.

ADOLESCENCE

This period lasts from about six months until about two years old (or until sexual maturity). During this time, the young fox's vision improves dramatically. They begin learning how to hunt on their own instead of relying solely on mommy dearest! They also learn how to coexist with other animals in their habitat — this includes both prey species as well as predators like wolves.

ADULTHOOD

After at least 2 years, a fox is considered a full-grown adult. At this stage, the fox has already mastered hunting on its own. They can now explore the world by themselves and are ready to have their own kits, too.

YOUR A __FUR__C__E__ TO BE RE__CK__ONED WITH!

LET'S HOWL THROUGH THE SOUNDS OF A FOX

Are you ready to hear the sound of a fox? Although you might think that foxes are silent creatures, they actually have several different noises they use to communicate with each other. The most common sound is a bark. Foxes also make growling noises and even hissing sounds if they feel threatened. They will also whine, yelp, yip, whimper, and make other sounds.

When a fox is happy and wants to show it off, it will *howl* like wolves. When it's scared, it will *yelp*. When it's angry at something or someone, it will *growl*. And when it wants something (*usually food*), it will *bark*! They also often make *hissing* noises when they are annoyed by something or someone nearby. These sounds are usually accompanied by raised hackles on their backsides as well as bared teeth and fur standing up around their neck area.

When asking for help, they will **bark** or *scream* on rare occasions. So, the next time you're out in the woods and hear sounds like these, you will know what they mean.

WHAT DO YOU CALL A FOX WHO LEADS AN EXPEDITION?

A <u>TAIL</u>-blazer!

THE IMPORTANCE OF FOXES

Foxes play a crucial role in the natural ecosystem — and we need to protect them. They are often underrated, and many people don't even know what they do.

The most important thing that foxes do is help keep rodents, mice, and insect populations under control. They do this by eating these critters that often damage crops if their numbers grow too high. If the population of these pests is not controlled, it would lead to more crop damage — not something we want for our dear farmers!

Foxes are also important because they are scavengers, eating animals that have died naturally or were killed by predators such as wolves or coyotes. This helps keep diseases from spreading among animals in the area.

HELP FOX SPECIES SURVIVE

Some fox species are at a higher risk of extinction because they have been hunted for their fur, which is used to make coats and accessories. Much of their wild habitat is also being destroyed to make room for more of us humans. One of the best ways you help foxes is to take care of their environment. Don't cut trees; instead, plant more trees! If you head out camping in the wild, remember to take home your trash.

Additionally, if you're lucky to see a fox around, don't make any move to hurt it. **Play it safe by watching them from afar.** Let them go on their own because they won't hurt you — unless you hurt them.

If we do our part in caring for the environment, we can make this world a better place to live for everyone.

THANK YOU FOR READING!

Foxes are among the most fascinating and crucial animals on our planet. We hope you have enjoyed learning more about them.

Remember that the learning doesn't end here! The more you learn about foxes, the more you can tell others about how important they are for the environment and how some species of foxes are endangered. You don't have to be an adult to make a difference! Every small bit helps foxes to thrive.

GO <u>FUR</u> IT!

THANK YOU!

Thank you for reading this book and for allowing us to share our love for foxes with you!

If you've enjoyed this book, please let us know by leaving a rating and a brief review wherever you made your purchase! This helps us spread the word to other readers!

Thank you for your time, and have an awesome day!

For more information, please visit:

www.animalreads.com

YOU GOT LOTS OF TAIL-LENT!

© Copyright 2022 - All rights reserved Admore Publishing

ISBN: 978-3-96772-125-6

ISBN: 978-3-96772-126-3

Animal Reads at www.animalreads.com

The content contained within this book may not be reproduced, duplicated or transmitted without direct written permission from the author or the publisher.

Under no circumstances will any blame or legal responsibility be held against the publisher, or author, for any damages, reparation, or monetary loss due to the information contained within this book. Either directly or indirectly.

Published by Admore Publishing: Gotenstraße, Berlin, Germany

www.admorepublishing.com

www.ingramcontent.com/pod-product-compliance
Lightning Source LLC
LaVergne TN
LVHW020142080526
838202LV00048B/3989